To Kant— avoid-the-lites! Debra Lindquist

I'm Sorry, You Didn't Tell Me You Were a VAMPIRE

Guidelines for Identifying Destructive Behavior in Ourselves and Others

Written By:
Debra Lindquist, M.A. | *Joyce Knudsen, Ph.D.*

Illustrations By:
Chris Wynkoop

Cover Design and Inside Layout By:
Amy Brenner Adams

Library of Congress Control Number: 2002091363
ISBN 0-9701744-2-X

Lindquist, Debra, MA, CIP
Knudsen, Joyce, Ph.D., CIM
I'm Sorry, You Didn't Tell Me You Were A Vampire
Color Profiles, Ltd.
The ImageMaker, Inc.

Printed in the USA by

MORRIS PUBLISHING

3212 East Highway 30   Kearney, NE 68847   1-800-650-7888

"Civility
costs nothing."

English Proverb

Table of Contents

Chapter One

How This Book Came to Be

Human beings have always tried to explain and to analyze patterns that they see in the behavior of others. When Debra saw the movie INTERVIEW WITH THE VAMPIRE, she found herself wondering why she was watching the movie. It was distasteful to her when two vampires, played by Brad Pitt and Tom Cruise, had an unquenchable need for blood. They went into the forest, made their human hits and sucked the blood from their victims. In pondering the incident, Debra decided that there was no reason for surprise. After all, these were vampire characters and the nature of vampires is to suck the blood of a victim.

There has been a fascination with the character of the vampire through the ages. Vampires have been perceived by the public as being sexy, dangerous, invincible and somewhat aristocratic. Authors Debra and Joyce decided to use the "vampire" as a vehicle for discussing human behavior in business and social relationships. They also extended the concept to include issues of etiquette. In real terms, no person is truly losing blood, but at times there is definitely a parallel to the concept of the personal vampire attack. We sometimes experience mini-vampire attacks. An individual may speak to us in a way that diminishes who we are. Their thoughtlessness is like a tiny dart that just for a brief moment inflicts a small wound.

> "Some cause happiness
> **wherever they go;**
> **others, whenever they go.**"
> Oscar Wilde

Through our lifetime we have a number of personal interactions with other people. We feel disappointed when the results of these interactions turn out to be slightly or extremely disastrous. We did not understand the nature of the person or people with whom we were dealing. We feel used or discarded as our energy has been dissipated. We feel powerless and fear that the blood has literally been sucked from our body. We wonder what happened. If only we would have known just what type of person we were dealing with, we could have been prepared. The parallel could be that we have experienced a vampire attack.

Not only do we experience vampire attacks, but we also may be behaving as vampires. This book will point out examples of vampire activity. If we are behaving as vampires by design, or without realizing it, we may choose to change our behavior. If we are experiencing "vampire attacks" we will recognize them for what they are because we will be more aware of the type of people with whom we are interacting. Our wounds will be expected and the attacks will not surprise us.

Freud, in his Three Essays on the Theory of Sexuality introduces the powerful rival emotions of love and hate. "The true prototypes of the relation of hate are derived not from sexual life, but from the ego's struggle to preserve and maintain itself." Hate, Freud explained, is older than love because hate's main priority is to preserve the self and to defend the ego from the external world, in fear that harm may come and, thus, threaten the ego's existence. Love, he says, is younger for it is an act of sharing the ego with the external world. People gain stability and defend themselves before they can trust the environment. This theory of hate can explain the behavior of people who feel they must hurt other people. From Freud's perspective, some crimes are committed with the emotion of hate and the goal of self-preservation; someone who could not consider loving others in their surrounding when their very existence is being jeopardized. This is the nature of the fictional "vampire" which by its very nature and need to survive must consume human blood. The "vampires" in our mind know the difference between right and wrong. Our deepest and darkest thoughts may invade us, but we "choose" to behave in a certain way.

Joyce Knudsen, Ph.D., is an Image Consultant and is an expert in personal and human psychological development. Debra Lindquist, MA, is also an Image Consultant. An unplanned quirk of fate brought the pair together at an Association of Image Consultants International Conference in Denver. This incident led to the discussion of vampire behavior.

Joyce and Debra share the belief system that business alliances and personal relationships should be based upon the "win-win" concept for all of the people involved. They share a point of view that there is never an appropriate reason to be spoken to in a negative, condescending or insensitive way.

The book is an effort to identify types of vampire behavior and to cite alternative options by showing people how to communicate without "sucking the blood" of their associates, friends or family. When you know the characteristics of "vampires" you will be able to analyze your own operational and behavioral style in order to see if you are using vampire techniques in interacting with others. You will be able to chart your own VAMPIRE BEHAVIOR QUOTIENT!

Some people have the concept of a "win-win" relationship when making alliances with others. They want good things to happen for themselves, and also want good things to happen for others as the result of the relationship. These people believe in the concept of the "unlimited larger pie." They think that there is "enough pie" for all involved.

> "If you can't be a good example, **then you'll just have to be a horrible warning.**"
>
> Catherine Arrd

Other people believe in the "fixed pie size" concept. There is only so much pie and a piece taken by another leaves less pie for them. These people are primarily self-serving and are usually not great people with whom to form alliances.

Sometimes people with this mind-set can masquerade as having a win-win point of view. However, when you work with them for a time the totally self-serving mentality that they have will surface.

All human actions are motivated. We need to learn to accept our own differences and the differences of others in order to avoid allowing them to become barriers to our success. We may not like how another chooses to behave, however, we cannot change the behavior of others. We can only change how we look at them and understand what drives them. People do things, or don't do things, for their own reasons. Research shows that we have all been genetically programmed to have this self-interest as a survival mechanism.

Understanding people and their needs is extremely important to the communication process. Understanding our behavior and our own needs is equally important. We all come from different environments and have our own experiences. It is inappropriate to "put down" another for our own self- aggrandizement. Our needs will be better served if we attempt to understand the other person's perspective. We also need to understand our own motives in dealing with others.

Many people feel that in their journey through life they

learn lessons in order to make them better people. The insight and personal growth that we experience, even as the result of unpleasant interactions with others, can make us more aware of how our behavior impacts those that we deal with in our daily lives.

This book will be organized by defining a particular type of vampire attitude or behavior. A Vampire Quotient Quiz For Vampire Tendencies to see if you are behaving like a vampire will follow this material. Strategies for this type of behavior will be included. The next quiz will be designed to analyze whether you have been "bitten" by a vampire. Strategies will follow for those who have been "bitten" by a vampire. In each chapter, the reader will have an opportunity to analyze whether they have a tendency towards the use of this behavior themselves, or whether they often find themselves interacting with people who use the behavior discussed in the chapter.

This book is intended to make us laugh at ourselves and recognize behaviors in ourselves and others that may be inappropriate in society. The key to better communication with people is to understand them. The more we understand our own behavior, the more secure we will become in our interaction with other people. The authors feel that in the final analysis, it is people and their feelings that matter the most. The Vampire Behavior Quotient Quizzes are informal tools to assist readers in thinking about how they are treated and even more important, how they are treating others.

#1

Chapter Two: Vampire Attitude

Anything You Can Do I Can Do Better

Joyce Knudsen, Ph.D., has noted that all people have the need to be acknowledged. They want to be viewed as being capable and significant. They want others to listen to them. They seek approval and hope to be cared about by others. They want to be protected and hope that other people will not exploit their vulnerabilities.

Superiority

Some people must be a bit better than anyone else on the planet. People that fit into this category like to think of themselves as being in the exclusive club called NUMBER I.

The vampire behavior that is operating here is definitely a

behavior of superiority. This superiority can be skill-based in that the person who feels superior often may be superior in many instances. Such a person who has an attitude of superiority must be certain that this attitude does not turn arrogant or elitist if the goal is working with other people.

"It's just not good enough" is the message of the person with the superior attitude when communicating to others. Such a technique is utilized to create the disempowerment of another person or associate. Whatever the person has done is not up to perceived standards. By raising the "limbo bar," the person with the "Just Not Good Enough" mentality always feels on top of the heap. The power hungry person's goal is to put people down in order to keep the position of "King or Queen of the Mountain."

"Words are **loaded pistols.**"

Jean-Paul Sartre

This personality type likes to criticize as it makes them feel more superior with their own work or ideas. The person who criticizes is merely "venting" as to how they would like the situation to be. There is no looking inside themselves to see why they have this need to be critical of others. This person believes that the "process" is more important than the "person" involved. Such a "vampire person" is not really interested in the opinions of those that they criticize.

Competition

Another operative behavior of this vampire attitude may be competition. People who are particularly competitive will go into a "competitive mode" anytime that they are working with others. Sometimes this competition will result in very productive efforts, but on other occasions the competition will be destructive rather than productive.

> **"When you win say nothing. When you lose, say less."**
> Paul Brown

Perfectionism

The person who is a perfectionist may possess this vampire attitude. A project will never be quite right, or the state of perfection that is necessary must only be rendered by the perfectionist's hand. Perfectionists are not satisfied with merely doing well or even with doing better than their peers. They are satisfied only if they have done a job perfectly so that the result reveals absolutely no blemishes or weakness of any kind as judged by their point of view. Perfectionists may strive for unreachable and complex goals. This behavioral type might be happiest when working alone. Perfectionists may cause problems for family members, coworkers, and associates who do not share the perfectionist's level of perfection.

> "If you are pleased with finding faults, you are displeased at finding perfection."
>
> Johan Laverty

Know It Alls

The "know it all" will also behave in a vampire-like fashion. Such a person may be highly intelligent and skilled. Even with such traits this person is often a disaster as an associate, co-worker, or friend. The effect of this type of personality shows a reluctance to call for help from anyone at anytime. Situations that could benefit from this person's

> "The dumbest people that I know are those who know it all."
>
> Malcolm Forbes

expertise may not be taken into consideration simply because nobody wants to deal with the know-it-all. This type of personality does not work well when teamwork is the goal of a company or organization.

"Know It All Vampire People" will not change their arrogance or overbearing personalities unless they choose to change.

"It's better to **know some** of **the questions** **than to know all of** the answers."

James Thurber

Vampire Quotient Quiz

for Vampire Tendencies

Anything You Can Do, I Can Do Better

Answer YES, NO, or SOMETIMES to any of the following questions. If the majority of your answers are YES, you may have vampire tendencies. If you feel that you do have vampire tendencies, don't let them get out of hand. Check the vampire strategies for suggestions if you are eager to curb your vampire tendencies.

1. I feel that my work is superior to most people and I let them know it.

   __ Yes __ No __ Sometimes

2. Few people that I work with have my level of technical competence.

   __ Yes __ No __ Sometimes

3. I just know more than most people.

   __ Yes __ No __ Sometimes

4. I judge people according to my standards.

   __ Yes __ No __ Sometimes

5. I would describe myself as being highly competitive.

__ **Yes** __ **No** __ **Sometimes**

6. I love to talk about the many things that I know about.

__ **Yes** __ **No** __ **Sometimes**

7. It is often "up to me" to take charge of most business situations.

__ **Yes** __ **No** __ **Sometimes**

8. I often have all the best ideas.

__ **Yes** __ **No** __ **Sometimes**

9. I find that the work of most people isn't up to my level of expectations.

__ **Yes** __ **No** __ **Sometimes**

Strategies for Dealing
with Vampire Behavior

Anything You Can Do, I Can Do Better

1. Analyze the basis for your feelings of superiority.
2. Pursue projects where you have the major responsibility.
3. Inform the team of your desire to contribute major input when it is necessary that you are a team member.
4. Establish guideline boundaries for yourself that are approved by team members.
5. A manager of a person with a definite superiority attitude and behavior may privately suggest the superiority person use more discretion when dealing with associates and co-workers.
6. Strive to appreciate the contributions of others through praise and recognition.
7. Explain to co-workers that you have a tendency to be very competitive.
8. Brainstorm with your team as to how your sense of competition will benefit the team.

9. Turn your competition switch to "off" when you sense that too much competition may be inappropriate.

10. Strive to become more aware in your sensitivity towards others.

11. Imagine how you might feel if faced with the possibility of dealing with a person who has your sense of superiority.

12. Analyze your need to be a perfectionist.

13. Are your levels of perfection required holding you back from achieving your goals?

14. If you are aware that you are a "know it all," limit your opinions to a few, rather than to every possible issue.

Vampire Quotient Quiz

If You've Been Bitten By a Vampire

Anything You Can Do, I Can Do Better

Answer YES, NO, or SOMETIMES to any of the following questions. Use the quiz below to evaluate if other people's behavior is affecting you and you feel as though you have been "bitten" by a vampire. If you answer YES to many of the questions it is possible that you lack self-confidence or feel intimidated by others. Check the strategies for dealing with "vampire bites" if you feel that you have been attacked by a vampire.

1. My work is often underrated.

   __ Yes __ No __ Sometimes

2. I am seldom given the opportunity to take charge in a group situation.

   __ Yes __ No __ Sometimes

3. People give me the impression that they know more than I do.

   __ Yes __ No __ Sometimes

4. I feel that my work is not appreciated by others.

__ Yes __ No __ Sometimes

5. People judge me according to “their” standards.

__ Yes __ No __ Sometimes

6. I am shy and don’t feel comfortable “tooting” my own horn.

__ Yes __ No __ Sometimes

7. I do my work, but I’m not going out of my way to be an overachiever.

__ Yes __ No __ Sometimes

8. I detest confrontations with others.

__ Yes __ No __ Sometimes

Strategies for Avoiding
Vampire Bites

Anything You Can Do, I Can Do Better

Review these strategies in order to see if you can learn how you may become more assertive in order to receive more attention for your work and your abilities.

1. Analyze the basis for the lack of attention of others towards you and the work that you do.

2. Let group members know that you are able and ready to contribute. Practice getting more involved.

3. If possible, choose to work with individuals who are more "user friendly" when working with others.

4. Avoid taking the comments of other people personally.

5. Explain to others that you react more favorably to a positive approach rather than a negative one.

6. Understand that people have different personalities and may not be tactful in many given situations.

7. Distance yourself from negative people and circumstances.

8. Upgrade your skills by attending classes.

9. Strive to excel in some area that you find to be of particular interest to you.

10. Learn to "speak up" for yourself and the work that you do. Various groups such as "Toast Masters" and other adult education groups promote speaking and improved communication.

11. Develop confidence in your work and in your abilities. If you are happy with your work, it is not necessary that others appreciate it.

12. Take charge, if you desire to do so, in group situations. Your right to be heard is equal to others in the group.

13. Respect over-achievers, even though you do not choose to be one.

14. Study information regarding confrontation. It is healthy to get out of your "comfort zone" at times.

Chapter Three: Vampire Attitude

Are We Having Fun Yet?

The vampire behavior that is operating here deals with the type of person who "won't be having fun." Some people with these attitudes use control tactics to keep their associates in limbo. One of the control tactics is the tactic of appearing to be dissatisfied with whatever the situation happens to be. These vampires will not jump to rectify the situation as being dissatisfied is too much fun.

High-Low Dispositions

These vampire people are unpredictable as to how they may feel and behave. You never know which way the happiness barometer will be pointing, as these people have a daily temperament that must be taken into consideration before having a conversation with them. They can be perfectly wonderful, fun, and funny one day and then completely irritated, critical, and irrational the next time that you see them. If they are in a position of power as a supervisor or committee chairman, their subordinates usually walk on eggshells in their presence. These vampire people are difficult to be around because you never know when they might "bite." They create an atmosphere of uncertainty for the people who are dealing with them. They may love your ideas and suggestions...or they may detest them. One never knows what their reaction will be. Their moodiness and emotional outbursts are their problems, not yours. Their outbursts are not personal; only self-inflicted. For whatever reason, they simply are not happy with themselves.

> "Everyone is perfectly willing to learn **from unpleasant experiences- if only the damage** of the first lesson **could be repaired.**"
>
> George Lichenberg

Insecurity

Sometimes these unhappy people will want to pass their own insecurities on to you. Maintain your power by not allowing this to happen. If you can laugh at the humor of the situation, or can appear to show no emotion, the attackers will see that they have failed to hurt you. If someone shows hostility towards you and you respond with humor, kindness or ignorance, the hostility of the attacker will be emphasized and they will appear even more childish and petty.

> "True success is the only thing that **you cannot have unless and until you have** offered it to others."
> Sri Chinmoy

Avoid responding to these vampires with anger. Maintain a non-aggressive even-tempered attitude. Kill the attackers with kindness, and echo what you think they are trying to communicate. Plan a strategy and avoid risking an "on the spot" confrontation with the attacking associate.

On occasion you may find that you have had long-term relationships with these vampires. You have totally misjudged the nature of your relationship and are quite surprised when these people have no alliance or loyalty towards you. Your vampire associate has exuded the behavior that everything is okay with your relationship. The truth happens to be that everything is far from okay. Since these vampires have a rather juvenile approach to life, it is not a surprise that they are unable to have deep, meaningful relationships. Don't rely on their long-term support and don't be dismayed when they let you down.

Vampire Quotient Quiz

for Vampire Tendencies

Are We Having Fun Yet?

Answer YES, NO, or SOMETIMES to any of the following questions. If the majority of your answers are YES, you may have vampire tendencies. If you answer NO to the majority of questions, it appears that you have an even temperament in dealing with others.

1. I have a difficult time being satisfied with what I am doing.

   __ Yes __ No __ Sometimes

2. I will often act satisfied even if I do not feel that way.

   __ Yes __ No __ Sometimes

3. I really never know how I'm going to feel.

   __ Yes __ No __ Sometimes

4. I will shift perceived alliances and loyalties to others if it is to my advantage to do so.

   __ Yes __ No __ Sometimes

5. I tend to be "up" and "down" in my moods.

__ **Yes** __ **No** __ **Sometimes**

6. I often think that I deserve more than I get.

__ **Yes** __ **No** __ **Sometimes**

7. I enjoy being perceived as being unpredictable.

__ **Yes** __ **No** __ **Sometimes**

8. I can't understand why some people seem so happy much of the time.

__ **Yes** __ **No** __ **Sometimes**

9. Selective people bare the brunt of my moods.

__ **Yes** __ **No** __ **Sometimes**

Strategies for Dealing
with Vampire Behavior

Are We Having Fun Yet?

1. Become aware of just what you are doing and try to discover why you are utilizing this type of behavior.

2. Is being a curmudgeon about everything really fulfilling?

3. What "pay off" do you receive when you appear to be happy, but are not happy at all?

4. Realize that you may be an "up" and "down" personality with your feelings and behavior. Try to document when these mood swings happen and why.

5. Is this type of behavior directed towards particular persons, or is it directed towards everyone?

6. Does diet, timely eating of meals, or exercise affect this mood swing process?

7. Is this type of behavior an effort to control others since they must encounter your "road block" of pain as they go about their daily lives?

8. Do you avoid "feeding in" to this behavior if you have a relationship with someone who utilizes these behavioral techniques?

9. Avoid trying to "fix" things for people who utilize this type of vampire behavior. People with these characteristics will "rain on your parade." Predict their moods and distance yourself from them when the moods are operative.

10. Does this type of behavior assist you in fulfilling your goals?

Vampire Quotient Quiz

If You've Been Bitten By a Vampire

Are We Having Fun Yet?

Answer YES, NO, or SOMETIMES to any of the following questions. Use the quiz below to evaluate how the behavior of others is affecting you. If you answer YES to any of these questions, you may be dealing with a vampire. You may also be extremely sensitive to the behavior of others. Their behavior may affect your well-being.

1. I am uncomfortable with moody people.

   __ Yes   __ No   __ Sometimes

2. I feel insecure when people say things to me that are hurtful.

   __ Yes   __ No   __ Sometimes

3. I prefer to be around happy people.

   __ Yes   __ No   __ Sometimes

4. I am not that fond of some of people that I know.

   __ Yes   __ No   __ Sometimes

5. If people don't treat me well, I will find some way to get even with them.

__ Yes __ No __ Sometimes

6. I feel that much unpleasant behavior is directed towards me.

__ Yes __ No __ Sometimes

Strategies for Avoiding
Vampire Bites

Are We Having Fun Yet?

1. Be sensitive and aware of the mood swings of others.
2. Use kindness in dealing with people who may be having a difficult day.
3. Speak up if someone is taking your power.
4. See if you are able to find any "humor" in the situation.
5. Do not allow anyone to create a social reality in your environment through their hostility.
6. Analyze whether you are taking your situation too seriously.
7. Decide whether there is any other situation in your life that is influencing your feelings.
8. When you attempt to interact with another, echo their operational style in your speech and manner.
9. Be aware that some people are moody. This is their personality type and if they choose to be "in a mood," do not allow yourself to be affected by their behavior.

10. Work on becoming more secure. Keep a journal and write positive entries about your daily successes. Eleanor Roosevelt said, "Nobody can make you feel insecure without your consent."

11. The saying, "Don't Get Mad, Get Even" has some truth to it for some people. Some people want revenge and are unforgiving. Forgive them.

Chapter Four: Vampire Attitude

You'll Do Until Something Better Comes Along

This type of vampire person makes an associate think that "a true working relationship" exists of camaraderie and support. The vampire person will appear to be quite engaging and of a "common mind" with an associate.

Master User

Actually, such a vampire is a "master user" of others. The charm factor is high in this "master user's" bag of tricks. Sometimes, this vampire is also perceived by others to be quite special or to be the type of person that would be "the one" to work with on a project. This vampire is particularly self-centered and feeds upon the attention of others. This vampire could even be quite competent as well as being a hard worker. Still, anything or anyone who will make this vampire "look good" is potential prey.

> "Conceit wouldn't be
> so terrible
> **if only the right**
> **people had it.**"
>
> Anonymous

Realize "up front" what a relationship with a person who fits this description and has these characteristics will produce. You may discover that it is better to "walk around" these people in order to achieve your goals.

Some people still may choose to be victims of the vampire's plots and schemes even when they know the probable results of the interaction. The short-term gratification that these people receive may be an adequate "pay off" for interacting with a vampire.

Some people believe in the basic laws of reciprocity. These laws state that people will reciprocate back to others comparable favors or things that have been extended to them. Good or bad behavior could be under consideration in our vampire's response to the laws of reciprocity. This vampire is primarily a "taker" and probably won't be a "giver" unless it is to the vampire's definite advantage.

Scanning

One technique that this vampire uses is the technique of "scanning" a variety of people. Scanning is looking over a group of people in order to decide who is the most powerful, most interesting, most influential, or most attractive. The scanner's goal is to make contact with this person. If you have ever been in a conversation with a "scanner" you know exactly what happens. The person you are speaking to appears to be listening but is scanning the room to see if someone who they perceive to be more important and more worthy of their attention is headed their way. These vampires are hoping to advance themselves by connecting with the people that they perceive to be most powerful.

Some "vampire people" are such masterful scanners that they can make you feel that you have their total attention in a conversation. These vampires may also be on a mission of gathering members of a particular group because of the perceived value that the group members will have in the vampire's "inner circle."

These vampires are very opportunistic. They appear to be giving their approval or agreement to you when you are interacting with them. What they say right now isn't necessarily what they will mean at a later time.

> "He who thinks himself wise,
> O heavens!
> is indeed a great fool."
> Voltaire

Networking

You may be wondering if networking is a type of scanning. Networking (communicating with many people) should be a more genuine form of communicating while scanning is primarily superficial. Networking is a term that we constantly hear about. Networking can be very effective in meeting a wide variety of people, learning about others, coming in contact with those who have your similar interests, as well as serving as an opportunity for marketing your services and products.

Vampire Quotient Quiz

for Vampire Tendencies

You'll Do Until Something Better Comes Along

Answer YES, NO or SOMETIMES to any of the following questions. YES answers may indicate that you have tendencies towards narcissistic behavior.

1. I'm interested in being with the "right" people.

   __ Yes **__ No** **__ Sometimes**

2. I'm good at supporting people until someone better comes along.

   __ Yes **__ No** **__ Sometimes**

3. I love to be with people who make me look good.

   __ Yes **__ No** **__ Sometimes**

4. I love to "work the room" in order to see who I can talk to in a social situation.

   __ Yes **__ No** **__ Sometimes**

5. I'm always looking for OPPORTUNITIES!

__ Yes __ No __ Sometimes

6. I may say something that I don't really mean in order to make an impression.

__ Yes __ No __ Sometimes

7. I am primarily attracted to BEAUTIFUL PEOPLE.

__ Yes __ No __ Sometimes

8. I feel more successful when I associate with those I perceive to be successful.

__ Yes __ No __ Sometimes

Strategies for Dealing
with Vampire Behavior

You'll Do Until Something Better Comes Along

1. Ask yourself if you have the need to bolster your own self esteem through your associations with others.

2. Try to determine why you are attracted to superficial people.

3. Document the agreements and interactions that you have with others. Do you want to be a person with integrity?

4. Remember that people will catch on to your superficiality and you won't be taken seriously.

5. Strive to adopt a "win-win" attitude with others. You will end up building more lasting relationships.

6. You will have to continually develop new circles of associates if you decide to pursue your current "vampire person" behavior.

7. Remember that the world doesn't revolve around YOU!

8. Practice being less "vampire like."

Vampire Quotient Quiz

If You've Been Bitten By a Vampire

You'll Do Until Something Better Comes Along

Answer YES, NO, or SOMETIMES to any of the following questions. Use this quiz to determine if the behavior of others is making you feel "bitten" by a vampire.

1. The people that I'd like to cultivate don't seem to be attracted to me.

   __ Yes __ No __ Sometimes

2. Some of the people I've tried to work with have ended up dropping me like a hot potato.

   __ Yes __ No __ Sometimes

3. I am uncertain which people to approach in a "cocktail party" setting.

   __ Yes __ No __ Sometimes

4. I am uncertain how to impress the people that I would really like to attract.

   __ Yes __ No __ Sometimes

5. I really don't know who I want to work with.

__ Yes __ No __ Sometimes

6. I probably am at my best when I work alone.

__ Yes __ No __ Sometimes

Strategies for Avoiding

Vampire Bites

You'll Do Until Something Better Comes Along

1. Seek out and associate with people who appreciate you for who you are.

2. Is there any justification as to why someone would drop you like a "hot potato?" If not, forget it and move forward.

3. Approach people at parties with a sense of spontaneity and fun. You might surprise yourself by who you meet.

4. The only person you have to impress is yourself. Be yourself and people will like you for who you are.

5. Appreciate the diversity of the different people you will meet in business. Understand their varying operational styles and they should also take the time to understand yours.

6. Realize the potential benefits of team environments.

7. Excuse yourself and leave the person you are speaking with if you sense that they are "scanning the room."

8. Some people may put their "foot in their mouth," and say something they really don't actually mean. Don't let their remarks hurt you. WALK AROUND these people in order to achieve your goals.

Chapter Five

I Am Powerful and You Are Under My Control

These vampires are masters of manipulation. They design their strategies in order to control others. Their tactics are many and are varied in order to achieve the results that they feel are important.

The types of manipulation that vampires use are based upon their own personal needs. Efforts to influence others should not be confused as necessarily being efforts of manipulation. The difference comes when the well-being of the other person involved in the interaction is considered. Vampire people focus exclusively on their intentions and wishes. "Win-win" outcomes for everyone should be the goal if the interactions are to be positive.

> "Nearly **all men** can stand **adversity,** but if you want to **test a man's character** give him power."
>
> Abraham Lincoln

George Simon is the author of the book, *In Sheep's Clothing*. In this book he describes manipulative behavior as "not being obvious." He says that our gut may tell us that manipulators are fighting for something, struggling to overcome us, gain power, or have their way, and we find ourselves unconsciously on the defensive. He states that, "Because we cannot point to clear objective evidence that manipulators are aggressing against us, we aren't readily validating our feelings."

Some vampires manipulate others for the purpose of self-enhancement. These vampires will try to get others to do particular work for them through trickery, charm, or by eliciting sympathy.

One way of manipulating others can be through the establishment of credentials. We've heard some individuals flaunt their levels of education. Other individuals feel that it is not only your education, but where you received that education that is critical. All of these techniques are attempts at creating elitist groups of credibility. In some instances these claims to fame are substantiated. Some individuals have received better educations from particular institutions. However, other factors of success are also operative in addition to the education factor.

People who provide information can also be critics of each other, establishing criteria that some information is better than other information. Some information can be perceived as being more authentic, more complete, more extensive, or more reliable than other information. A vampire technique is that of discrediting competitors who also provide similar information.

Some vampires "piggy back" upon the concepts and hard work of others. These "take charge" vampires use this type of manipulation to convince another that their "vampire seal of approval" is absolutely essential for the success of the other person's project. Again, if it is not a "win-win" situation for both parties involved, someone is being taken advantage of through the process of intimidation.

We all have our own energy to spend on whatever efforts we choose to pursue. Even though there is no limit to the energy we can appear to have, some people appear to be more energetic than others. Vampires find high energy levels in others very appealing. Not only do they want to figuratively "suck your blood," they want to suck your energy as well.

Vampire Quotient Quiz

for Vampire Tendencies

I Am Powerful and You Are Under My Control

Answer YES, NO, or SOMETIMES to any of the following questions. If you currently use any of these behaviors in your relationships, mark YES.

1. I enjoy the feeling of power and use it to my advantage.

   __ **Yes** __ **No** __ **Sometimes**

2. Most of my business transactions are structured so that I have the power to make the final decisions.

   __ **Yes** __ **No** __ **Sometimes**

3. People tell me that I can be manipulative.

   __ **Yes** __ **No** __ **Sometimes**

4. I am primarily concerned with my own well-being.

   __ **Yes** __ **No** __ **Sometimes**

5. I love taking on a project when there is a great worker on my team.

__ **Yes** __ **No** __ **Sometimes**

6. I think of myself as the "director" of most projects

__ **Yes** __ **No** __ **Sometimes**

7. My philosophy is that most people need to be told what to do.

__ **Yes** __ **No** __ **Sometimes**

8. I don't really think of myself as "bossy." I just have most of the best ideas.

__ **Yes** __ **No** __ **Sometimes**

Strategies for Dealing
with Vampire Behavior

I Am Powerful and You Are Under My Control

1. Be more aware as to why you behave as you do. Are you also empowering others? Try spreading the power around.

2. Do you miss opportunities of working with some competent people because they perceive that you will attempt to rob them of their power?

3. Is it necessary that people "work for you" rather than "work with you?"

4. Do others try to "rob you of your power" by discrediting your contributions, talents and work?

5. Have you been "burned" in your life by people that you perceive to be more powerful than you?

6. Is it always necessary for you to be talking about yourself and your projects? Do you take time to hear about the "power roles" of others?

7. Analyze your own manipulation techniques. Make certain that there is fair value for the other person.

Vampire Quotient Quiz

If You've Been Bitten By a Vampire

I Am Powerful and You Are Under My Control

Answer YES, NO, or SOMETIMES to any of the following questions. Use the quiz below to evaluate how the behavior of others is affecting you. If the majority of your answers are YES, you need to discover how to achieve your own power.

1. I really don't feel like I have much power at all.

   __ Yes __ No __ Sometimes

2. I don't have an ability to Influence others.

   __ Yes __ No __ Sometimes

3. I tend to think of myself as more of a follower rather than a leader.

   __ Yes __ No __ Sometimes

4. Sometimes I feel that my talents and ideas are "used" by others.

   __ Yes __ No __ Sometimes

5. I prefer direction from others when I am working on a project.

__ **Yes** __ **No** __ **Sometimes**

6. I would like to develop more confidence and more personal power.

__ **Yes** __ **No** __ **Sometimes**

Strategies for Avoiding
Vampire Bites

I Am Powerful and You Are Under My Control

1. Learn to identify the wide variety of manipulation techniques and tactics used by these vampires. Sometimes these tactics may not be immediately apparent.

2. Analyze the pay off of being in an association with a perceived person of power if the end result will not produce a "win-win" situation for you.

3. If you consent to be manipulated by another, be certain that you know what is in it for you.

4. If you think that you are dealing with a self-serving manipulator, make certain that you think through the situation carefully before making any commitments to such an individual.

5. Do your research. Don't let the self-serving manipulator do a number on you.

6. Remember that your energy is limited. Use it wisely for situations that benefit you.

Chapter Six: Vampire Attitude

Be Careful, I Gotcha

This type of vampire person loves to hinder the progress of others. Vampire people of this nature will continually dream up ways to impede the progress that others are trying to make. The attitude is actually a control technique because the vampire people are "in the driver's seat." They are in charge of making the final decision. These vampires want to have the last word and it may be impossible to thwart their authority.

You may think of these "gotcha vampires" as carrying around huge gold "NOT APPROVED" stamping seals. They love to use the stamping seals whenever they can.

Encounters with these Vampire people may cause others mountains of stress.

We all meet these vampire types in every phase of our lives, from our most simplistic activities to those activities that are far more complex. You might think of the many times that you've been at the post office and have wondered if anyone there had ever heard of the term, "Customer Service."

It may be the lunch hour, and lots of people are standing in line to mail letters and packages. These people are approaching the counters that could allow five postal workers to process the letters and packages. For some reason, only two postal workers are processing mail behind the counters.

The reason could be that the manager of the particular post office feels that the workers are needed in other parts of the post office. These managers may not realize the high need in the mailing section of the post office. Wouldn't it be wonderful if three more postal workers could be found in order to process the line more effectively? The majority of postal workers are extremely effective, are very pleasant and work diligently to serve the public. There are those postal workers who give you the feeling that they are government workers who cannot be fired. Their body language and behavior communicates that they are going to do whatever they feel like doing in their own time. Such vampire-like behavior also exists within other fields and is not just an issue at the post office.

Suppose that you are striving to fulfill some particular requirements for an award or advancement. You assemble the information and material that you perceive to be required. Somehow, the person who reviews your material finds that you have neglected to include some obscure portion of the requirement, which means that it is back to the drawing board for you. Again, this is not to say that requirements are unimportant. Some vampire people are overly particular, when the level of being particular enough has been met. The above described incident could be quickly handled with more help and support from the person reviewing the requirements.

> "There is no such thing as a problem without a gift for you in it's hands. You seek problems because you **need the gifts.**"
>
> Richard Bach

Vampire Quotient Quiz

for Vampire Tendencies

Be Careful, I Gotcha

Answer YES, NO, or SOMETIMES to any of the following questions. If you currently use any of these behaviors in your relationships, mark YES.

1. Control over others and their activities is very important to me.

   __ Yes __ No __ Sometimes

2. Rules are very important to me. I enjoy enforcing them.

   __ Yes __ No __ Sometimes

3. I think that people get too "cocky" if things come to them too easily.

   __ Yes __ No __ Sometimes

4. "No pain, no gain," has always been my philosophy.

   __ Yes __ No __ Sometimes

5. I've had to work for everything I have ever gotten. Why shouldn't everyone else do the same.

__ Yes __ No __ Sometimes

6. I think that "customer service" is a joke. I believe that the customer is not always right.

__ Yes __ No __ Sometimes

7. I love having the last word.

__ Yes __ No __ Sometimes

8. I believe things should be structured.

__ Yes __ No __ Sometimes

9. I could have done a lot better in my life if I would have had the opportunities that some people have had in their lives.

__ Yes __ No __ Sometimes

10. I would say that I am not a "risk taker."

__ Yes __ No __ Sometimes

Strategies for Dealing *with Vampire Behavior*

Be Careful, I Gotcha

1. Determine why it is important for you to have control over others.

2. Do you assist those who need to improve in order to get your approval?

3. Be more sensitive when you note an individual's frustration and stress in dealing with a "gotcha" situation.

4. Examine whether your own lack of personal success makes you enjoy holding others back.

5. Do you feel that your own personal struggles to become successful make you want to see other people struggle to? If so, it's time to re-examine.

6. Think about whether you might be bored with your job or career. If you are, this could be a reason that you want to "bite" someone.

7. Do you feel that your working efforts go unheralded? Is your vampire behavior a way of getting back at others?

8. Are your own personal successes more important than the successes of others? If you believe this, you may be using "gotcha behavior" and you don't even realize it.

Vampire Quotient Quiz

If You've Been Bitten By a Vampire

Be Careful, I Gotcha

Answer YES, NO, or SOMETIMES to any of the following questions. Use the quiz below to evaluate if the behavior of others is affecting you. YES answers will indicate that you have been "bitten." Refer to the Strategies for avoiding "vampire bites."

1. I experience much frustration in getting things accomplished. Someone always seems to block my progress.

   __ Yes __ No __ Sometimes

2. I often encounter a number of unpleasant people who are not interested in helping me.

   __ Yes __ No __ Sometimes

3. So much of my time is spent on frustrating tasks and activities.

   __ Yes __ No __ Sometimes

4. People often take their feelings of anger out on me.

__ **Yes** __ **No** __ **Sometimes**

5. I don't strive for rewards or advancements. It just takes more effort than it is worth.

__ **Yes** __ **No** __ **Sometimes**

6. My relatives always told me that I wouldn't amount to much. (OUCH!!)

__ **Yes** __ **No** __ **Sometimes**

Strategies for Avoiding
Vampire Bites

Be Careful, I Gotcha

Review these strategies to see if better organization and more assertive action towards others will help you avoid vampire "bites."

1. Evaluate your level of self-esteem. You can do this by making inventories regarding your self-esteem, by reading books on the topic, or you may wish to consider enrolling in a class in order to explore concepts of self-esteem.

2. Decide if your services have usually been relegated to what you consider to be unimportant tasks. If this is true, why do you believe it to be so?

3. Do not allow stronger people to take advantage of you.

4. If you are not getting the satisfaction you are seeking, perhaps it would be better to find a situation where you can meet this need.

5. Structure your work and activities in order to avoid frustrating encounters with others.

6. If you work in a bureaucracy, know that this "gotcha" vampire personality may surface at some point. Be prepared for the attack.

7. Put yourself in a mind-set to recognize "gotcha vampire behavior."

8. Ask yourself if any "gotcha" vampire behavior is about the "gotcha vampire" or about you. Usually, the vampire is at fault.

9. Keep in mind that you will be unable to control the behaviors of others.

10. Allow extra time when dealing with the "gotcha vampire." Avoid personal stress in the situation.

Chapter Seven: Vampire Attitude

Are You An Amplifier or An Admonisher?

The concept of "spin" is one that we know about because we hear about it on the news broadcasts and read about it in publications. Clever reporters and storytellers can create a story that in no way resembles the actual happening.

Amplifiers

People who are amplifiers are similar to those who put a "spin"on the statements they make. Amplifiers may not be telling a real lie, but they often reinvent the story to be taken in an entirely different way. When amplifiers are on your side, they can be very supportive. When you hear them talking about how fantastic you are, or about what you've done it is almost unbelievable that they are speaking about you. You are pleased to hear the wonderful patter because the story line makes you sound terrific.

Amplifiers use words, inflections and facial expressions to communicate their concepts. They are often very persuasive as well, and speak as though they should be believed. They are master presenters of the information that they choose to impart.

> "We always **weaken** when we **exaggerate.**"
>
> Anonymous

A clever line from a movie comes to mind. An attorney make the comment, "I could tell a story that would make Mother Theresa appear unfit to care for children." Since the majority of people know that Mother Theresa's life work involved the care of children, the very thought of such a statement seems ludicrous. The way one tells the story is the key to getting the desired reactions from others.

The vampire side of the amplifier comes when destruction becomes the mode and the amplifier goes after your juggler vein. The same skillful tactics are used to make the vampire amplifier's case. Great destruction can occur as a result of this vampire's work.

We all know terrific salespeople who are able to make something quite ordinary sound much more appealing than it is in reality. We often enjoy this type of selling process, because it "romances" our purchase and we feel good about it. We move right along with the seller in creating mental pictures about how wonderful our purchase is and how much we will enjoy having made the purchase.

This type of selling technique may be viewed as persuasive selling. The seller is amplifying whatever needs to be amplified in order to make the sale. This type of selling can be effective if the seller is not only selling, but is also considering the needs and wishes of the person being sold. If the deal is only a good deal for the seller, then it is not a "win-win" for both parties involved.

Sometimes, the sale does not involve a product or piece of merchandise, but may involve the sale of an idea or concept. This is where persuasive selling may actually turn in to a type of negative manipulation. The selling amplifier will insinuate a situation without totally spelling it out as it exists. Years ago, there was a physician who had a sign in his office that read, "What You Think You Are Hearing Me Say, May Not Be What I Am Saying At All." The words of this sign often come to mind when pondering the concept of the influential amplifier.

> "Whoever gossips to you will gossip of you."
> Spanish Proverb

Gossips and Rumor Spreaders

Gossips and spreaders of rumors are first cousins of the amplifier vampires. While the majority of the amplifier's information may contain more truth, the gossips and rumor spreaders may decide not to include truth at all.

There is a fine line concerning gossip. A clever poster showed four women talking. The poster had the caption, "We're Not Gossiping, We're Networking." We all love to get new information, hear a scoop and know what is going on. When is conversation defined as gossip? That is a difficult question to ponder as there are so many ramifications that must be considered. Sometimes, when people may appear to be gossiping, they are just exchanging their own feelings and perceptions. If we have an innate curiosity about many things, we may be inclined towards an exchange of information.

People who gossip and spread rumors will deliberately seek out those who are eager and ready to hear the latest gossip. Give the person in question the "benefit of the doubt," when you hear someone gossiping or exaggerating the facts. Hear the "other side of the story" in order to have the entire picture.

The Admonishing Vampire

The admonishing vampire struggles with a need to control situations by monitoring people and events. This vampire does not "go with the flow" and may have difficulty dealing with those that do. The admonishing vampire has a high need for structure and wants to make certain that rules of structure are followed. This vampire is frustrated when situations or the behavior of others does not proceed on track as planned.

> "It's not enough that we do our best; sometimes we have to do what's required."
>
> Winston Churchill

The admonishing vampire wants to know how things are progressing and how they will turn out. The admonishing vampire wants guarantees. This type of vampire may be trying to be very helpful as it appears that effort is being put towards keeping people and events rolling. The admonishing vampire actually saps the energies from others by admonishing them. This vampire may perceive the admonishment of others as being an empowering technique.

Vampire Quotient Quiz

for Vampire Tendencies

Are You An Amplifier or An Admonisher?

Answer YES, NO or SOMETIMES to any of the following questions. If the majority of your answers are YES, you may have need to consult the strategies section for improving this type of vampire behavior.

1. I intend to have my information taken at face value.

   __ Yes __ No __ Sometimes

2. I have a tendency to exaggerate and amplify.

   __ Yes __ No __ Sometimes

3. I like to be in control of situations.

   __ Yes __ No __ Sometimes

4. I just do not consider the expectations of others.

   __ Yes __ No __ Sometimes

5. When I give information, people need to listen.

   __ Yes __ No __ Sometimes

6. I have a passion for procedures and rules.

__ Yes __ No __ Sometimes

7. I enjoy creating my own reality when I tell a story.

__ Yes __ No __ Sometimes

8. I am a master at influencing and convincing others.

__ Yes __ No __ Sometimes

9. I consider myself a phenomenal sales person.

__ Yes __ No __ Sometimes

10. I will reword the facts to get people to listen to me.

__ Yes __ No __ Sometimes

Strategies for Dealing
with Vampire Behavior

Are You An Amplifier or An Admonisher?

1. Be aware of what you are saying. You may be an amplifier.
2. Understand that your thinking regarding amplifying and admonishing may differ from the thinking of others.
3. Realize that most people want to be "heard" rather than just "sold."
4. It is not your job to monitor people and events.
5. Know that sometimes things will not proceed on track as you plan and expect.
6. Practice "going with the flow" when you are interacting with other people.
7. Realize that you are sapping the energy of others when you admonish them.
8. Listen to the other people in a group. You will learn something.
9. Work more as a team mate; not the entire team.
10. Understand that when you admonish others you do not empower them.

Vampire Quotient Quiz

If You've Been Bitten By a Vampire

Are You An Amplifier or An Admonisher?

Answer YES, NO, or SOMETIMES to any of the following questions. Use this quiz to determine if the behavior of others is making you feel "bitten" by a vampire.

1. Some people tell me stories that are difficult to believe.

   __ Yes __ No __ Sometimes

2. I've been told that I have a tendency to be gullible in believing anything I hear.

   __ Yes __ No __ Sometimes

3. I am aware that some of the people I know who like to gossip are spreading gossip about me.

   __ Yes __ No __ Sometimes

4. I don't know why I buy some of the things I buy. I think that it is easy to sell me things, even if I really don't want them.

   __ Yes __ No __ Sometimes

5. I tend to allow people to gossip to me because it makes me feel like a special confident.

__ **Yes** __ **No** __ **Sometimes**

6. If some people I know would stop "monitoring me" I would accomplish more.

__ **Yes** __ **No** __ **Sometimes**

7. People tend to take undeserved credit for my accomplishments.

__ **Yes** __ **No** __ **Sometimes**

Strategies for Avoiding
Vampire Bites

Are You An Amplifier or An Admonisher?

1. You do not need to be monitored and you should not monitor others.

2. Remember that it is your choice to allow another to rob you of your energy.

3. Let your expectations be known and avoid the control of others in any given situation.

4. Establish boundaries for your behavior and stick with these boundaries that you establish.

5. Rely on your intuition when dealing with an amplifier. Once you have identified this person, you can know what to expect.

6. Avoid committing more than you can deliver to an admonisher.

7. Understand that the admonisher needs to adhere to rules and regulations. This is a respectable behavior if it does not infringe upon your beliefs.

8. Be aware of the exaggerations of others. Do your own research.

9. Put your ideas on the table so that others will know how you feel. Cooperate in the spirit of teamwork.

10. Establish your own boundaries of "truth" when you are dealing with an amplifier.

Chapter Eight: Vampire Attitude

Vampire People You Really Love to Hate

Some people that you "love to hate" may be guilty of behaving like vampires. They often aren't totally aware of their own behavior and its effect upon others. They are usually so focused upon themselves that they seldom think of how their actions impact others.

Time Abuser Vampires

The issue of time comes to mind as a key area of "vampire activity." Time is an unusual phenomenon in our society. We all have the same twenty four hours of time each day, but many of us are concerned as to how to use this time to our advantage. We value time well spent. We are looking for time continually. We never have enough time and we are concerned about how we spend our time. We will pay to spend time with others if they offer us benefits that we perceive to be of value.

Concepts of time are also viewed to be cultural in nature. Some countries are so time conscious that "being on time" is a major value of all operations in the country. Other cultures really don't view time with such a high level of importance. They do things when they get around to doing them and don't feel badly because of their decisions.

Lois Levy, author of ***Undress Your Stress***, suggests that time as we know it is completely artificial with various time zones including such concepts as daylight savings time. She talks about "racing against the clock," "trying to find time," "making time," "running out of time," and "making up for lost time," as concepts that will only drive us crazy if we choose to let them do so.

Vampires have all of the time in the world since they have the potential of living forever. Vampires like to play with concepts of time. One example of vampire behavior is the time waster who is always late. This Vampire values his or her time, but not YOUR TIME.

Vampires like this feel that all that is necessary is, "Sorry that I'm late." If such an expression makes your blood boil, you've just been attacked by a vampire. Vampires always think primarily of themselves. They may choose to be totally irresponsible about issues of time.

If you see a bit of the vampire in yourself regarding issues of time, you may want to take some time to examine the topic. How you utilize your time in your business will help you grow your business, or will cut your business down before it blooms. Your personal and professional relationships will run more smoothly if you address issues of time.

> "Without the management of time, you will soon have nothing left to manage."
>
> William D. Reiff

Talking Vampires

Other vampires you may love to hate are those that you perceive as talking too much. Some people are uncomfortable with long periods of silence when they are interacting with others. However, nothing is more frightening than the "vampire bore" who once engaged in conversation starts running off at the mouth and won't let anyone else get a word in edgewise. This vampire is waiting to talk. A tape is running in the vampire's head of the words and sentences that will be spewed to the vampire's victim.

The talking vampire may be one who finishes the sentences of others before they can get a word in edgewise. This vampire does not consider asking questions when engaged in conversation. The vampire has center stage and continues in non-stop conversation. Most people interacting with such a vampire person respond with a nodding head, and keep an ear out for a possible exit time.

"The greatest gift you can give another is the purity of your attention."
Richard Moss

Another type of vampire that talks excessively is the vampire person who calls you on the telephone just to talk. These people want to talk, have lots of time to talk, and usually feel better after they have been talking. Often, their conversations are completely self-focused and they are probably thinking, "Let me see what I have not told you about myself?" They have already related the messages, but take delight in repeating them. When you are talking to these vampire people, you can almost literally leave the telephone. Upon your return you would discover that these people are still talking about themselves. This vampire person calls at a time convenient for them and assumes that this time is also convenient for you to listen to their problems, challenges and life situations.

They blame others for the situations that they find themselves experiencing, and praise their own talents and efforts for their justifications. These vampire people who talk on the phone seldom solve many of the problems that they talk about. They just need to be heard and are looking for an ear to hear them.

Talking vampire people may become obsessive about some new activity or product that they are promoting. They will tell you over and over again about the concept in which they are interested. Their intent is to get you to buy or promote the concept too. They are using the principle of repetition with the hope that you will finally believe what they are saying.

Vampire Button Pushers

Some people are allergic to particular foods like peanuts and shellfish. These people become violently ill when they come into contact with these foods. These people have had their "physical health and well-being buttons" pushed by exposure to these substances.

Vampires are perceptive and can make remarks that push your "psychological well-being buttons." These chameleon vampires have the perceptions to identify chinks in the psychological armor of another. The vampires will zone in on the weakness areas with comments that are definitely "button pushers." The best way to avoid Vampire Button Pushers is to identify them and make them aware of the games that they are playing. If you can't avoid them and must interact or work with them, train yourself to walk around their button pushing behavior.

The Backstabber Vampire

Be very cautious once you have identified a vampire backstabber. These vampire people can never be trusted. They often appear to be wonderful people who could possibly be your dearest friends and supporters. They are the type of persons who say one thing to your face and another behind your back, betraying your confidence. Backstabbing often occurs when a person agrees with you when the two of you are together and later sides with your opponents when you are not present. Backstabber vampires will never miss an opportunity to backstab. They always have a little barb to throw to anyone who will catch it.

"Trust not him
with your secrets who,
when left alone in your room,
turns over your papers."

Johann Lavater

The Copy Cat Vampire

It is often said that imitation is the greatest form of flattery. We all know that there are few totally original ideas. Everyone is inspired from some other source. Often less creative people will jump upon another's concept or idea and will play it to the hilt. The Copy Cat Vampire is on the loose to snare and use any ideas that can be garnered from others. This vampire usually doesn't give credit to another for the unique concepts that are pilfered or are misrepresented. The Copy Cat Vampire is often very self-righteous and gives the feeling that "Copy Cat behavior" isn't even an option for any of his or her behavior patterns.

In order to avoid being a "Copy Cat Vampire" give credit where credit is due, and watch how you handle the information that you get from others.

Vampire Quotient Quiz

for Vampire Tendencies

Vampire People You Really Love to Hate

Answer YES, NO, or SOMETIMES to any of the following questions. If the majority of your answers are YES, you may have vampire tendencies. If you feel that you do have vampire tendencies, consult the strategies for dealing with this behavior.

1. I am often slightly late for many of my engagements.

   __ Yes __ No __ Sometimes

2. My friends expect me to be late and don't seem to mind.

   __ Yes __ No __ Sometimes

3. I find it difficult to plan my time effectively.

   __ Yes __ No __ Sometimes

4. I have so many things to do that the time runs out before I know it.

__ Yes __ No __ Sometimes

5. I love to talk and all the people I know are interested in what I have to say.

__ Yes __ No __ Sometimes

6. When I'm talking to someone else I'm usually thinking about myself.

__ Yes __ No __ Sometimes

7. I can always sell other people on things that I'm promoting.

__ Yes __ No __ Sometimes

8. Sometimes my friends seem very upset with me, and I really don't know why they should be.

__ Yes __ No __ Sometimes

9. I find it difficult to say what I want to say to someone's face. I don't like confrontations.

__ **Yes** __ **No** __ **Sometimes**

10. If I feel wronged by another person, I'll get back at them.

__ **Yes** __ **No** __ **Sometimes**

11. I get the best ideas from looking at other people's work.

__ **Yes** __ **No** __ **Sometimes**

Strategies for Dealing
with Vampire Behavior

Vampire People You Really Love to Hate

1. Think about the concept of time and how you feel about it. Treat others with the importance they deserve by being on time.

2. Take into consideration that being on time for appointments and commitments is a value that you should consider.

3. Try to pinpoint the reasons why you are often late.

4. Try adding fifteen extra minutes to your time frame. See if the cushion of time assists you in being punctual.

5. Vow to give a little gift each time that you are late for anyone and keep them waiting. When you get tired of giving free gifts, you'll be on time.

6. Ask other people questions about themselves when you are talking to them.

7. Check with your caller in order to see that your telephone call is coming at an appropriate time.

8. The majority of your phone calls should be limited to a short time period. Don't assume that the person receiving your call has all of the time in the world to talk.

9. Don't use the principle of "over kill" in getting your points across when you are promoting a product or a service.

10. Remember what Thumper the rabbit said in "Bambi." "If you can't say something nice, don't say nothing at all."

11. People appreciate your behavior when you acknowledge them.

Vampire Quotient Quiz

If You've Been Bitten By a Vampire

Vampire People You Really Love to Hate

Answer YES, NO, or SOMETIMES to any of the following questions. Use the quiz to evaluate if other people's behavior is making you feel "bitten" by a vampire. Resolve to take steps and use strategies that will help you gain the attention and respect that you deserve.

1. My blood boils when people are late for an appointment with me.

   __ Yes   __ No   __ Sometimes

2. People don't seem to understand how important time is to me.

   __ Yes   __ No   __ Sometimes

3. Most people I know seem primarily focused on themselves.

   __ Yes   __ No   __ Sometimes

4. I become easily bored with most people's conversations.

__ Yes __ No __ Sometimes

5. People telephone me "just to talk" when I am busy.

__ Yes __ No __ Sometimes

6. I find that I can't trust many people.

__ Yes __ No __ Sometimes

7. I don't know how to respond when some people say unkind things about others.

__ Yes __ No __ Sometimes

8. I am afraid that I will hurt other people's feelings.

__ Yes __ No __ Sometimes

9. I wish that I could promote myself the way that some people promote themselves.

__ Yes __ No __ Sometimes

Strategies for Avoiding

Vampire Bites

Vampire People You Really Love to Hate

1. Confirm meeting times with others. Make it very clear that you expect "on time" appointments.

2. Tell people you are meeting that you will expect a telephone call if they are running late. Make certain that they have your telephone number.

3. Divert others into two way conversations by asking them questions that require an answer that is not about them.

4. Allow a certain amount of time to listen to people who need to vent or to "let it all out" if these people are important to you.

5. Avoid being taken in by the "backstabber." Do not confide in this vampire type.

6. Stand up for the victims of the "backstabber" by saying something nice about the victim. Always say nice things about others to others.

7. Make a positive impression on the people you meet. These people will be less likely to believe things about you that they hear from a "backstabber."

8. Avoid being affected by people who push your buttons. Listen to what they say. Repeat what they are saying, but do not react until you have time to think about a strategy that you will use in dealing with them.

9. Document the work that you do in order to avoid Copy Cat Vampire types of people.

10. Make it very clear when you are not interested in participating in some other person's marketing scheme, or in someone's concept of product or service promotion.

Chapter Nine: Vampire Attitude

Discounting Manners

Everyone responds to good manners. Human beings respond in a positive fashion to other human beings who treat them with respect. We have read stories about vampires who have used "good manners" as part of the seduction process of their victims. Good manners can and usually will seduce even the most jaded of individuals. We feel better about our interactions with others when we are treated with respect. It would be optimum if sincerity accompanied good manners. We appear to be more sincere to others when we practice and use good manners.

"You can tell a great deal about a person's upbringing by the way he treats the help, his subordinates at the office and his competition in the marketplace."

Ruth Kern- International Etiquette Consultant

Eating

Eating is something that we are all involved in doing every day of the year. We should be masters at using the best of manners when eating alone (for our own civility), but we should pay particular attention when eating with others. Our behavior when eating definitely affects the dining experience of a companion or companions.

First of all, know the basics of using the correct utensils in the proper manner. This information is readily available in any number of etiquette books that you may choose to buy or may secure from a library.

If you are preparing and presenting food to others keep in mind the esthetics of creating an attractive presentation. A placemat, attractive napkin and a napkin ring will give the diner a feeling that some thought has gone into the event. The food is the final statement and should also be attractively presented.

The stage has been set for a dining experience. Try not to spoil the effect with poor table manners or by grabbing for your companion's food because you want to taste it. Request an extra plate and serving spoon from your waiter only if sharing of food is part of the dining plan.

Sound is part of the total package of dining. Avoid smacking, snorting, or other unpleasant noises. Some people find "blowing your nose at the table" to be offensive.

Eat as though you don't have a "racing stripe" on your fork. Savor your food and put your fork down occasionally while you are eating. Model the pace of your dining partner. Avoid gobbling your food quickly and appearing uneasy while your dining partner completes the meal. When you are finished eating, place your utensils on your plate so that the waiter knows you are ready for them to clear the table.

"The world is my oyster
but I used the wrong fork."
Oscar Wilde

TOP TEN DINING MISTAKES

1. Talking with food in your mouth.

2. Picking your teeth.

3. Elbows on the table.

4. Leaving belongings on the table.

5. Poor posture.

6. Using cell phones.

7. Eating too fast or too slow.

8. Pushing away the plate.

9. Playing with your hair.

10. Speaking too loudly.

(List is courtesy of Sue Fox, *Etiquette for Dummies*)

Family Friends and Co-Workers

The statement, "Familiarity Breeds Contempt" may turn out to be true when we are dealing with those people who are in our immediate circles of activity. Even though we are well-meaning, the day to day proximity with these people can be nerve wracking. We know their faults and they know ours. The stress of everyday living may cause us to treat these people with less respect than we would show to strangers. Often these people will be our most valuable allies. Give some thought to using better manners in dealing with these people in order to make them feel special and valued.

> "The best way to knock a chip off someone's shoulder is to pat them on the back."
>
> Anonymous

Travel

We may forget our manners when we are away from home and the surroundings of familiarity. Sometimes the opposite is true, and our manners may even improve when we are in a new environment. We often encounter stressful situations when we travel. We desperately want our travel experiences to be successful. It could be easy to explode with harsh demanding complaints when things are not to our expectation and liking. After all, we are also "paying" for the experience. Workers in the travel industry will assist us much more graciously when we treat them with respect and when we are generous with our kindness to them.

Road Rage

In this day and age there are more "vampires" behind the wheel. They are often running late, are in a rush and are anxious to reach their destinations at any cost.

The sports utility vehicle has empowered many drivers with "army like" armor to move down the highway with little regard for other drivers. These large vehicles block the views of other drivers as they may aggressively take more than their share of the road. Sports utility vehicles have their place and their function, but their popularity necessitates a new breed of manners on the highway.

Drivers of all automobiles should not make obscene gestures at other motorists nor should they shout comments and deliver "ugly looks" to fellow drivers. It would be wonderful to find happier, more thoughtful drivers behind the wheel.

Vampire Quotient Quiz

for Vampire Tendencies

Discounting Manners

Answer YES, NO, or SOMETIMES to any of the following questions. If the majority of your answers are YES, you may have vampire tendencies. You may wish to rethink your behavior as vampire tendencies could be impeding your success.

1. I like to relax when I eat, and I don't want to be bothered thinking about my behavior.

   __ Yes __ No __ Sometimes

2. I put my purse and reading glasses on the table in order to keep track of where they are.

   __ Yes __ No __ Sometimes

3. I don't want to miss my telephone calls just because I'm eating.

   __ Yes __ No __ Sometimes

4. If I'm in a bad mood, I'll probably take it out on my family or on others.

__ **Yes** __ **No** __ **Sometimes**

5. It's my right to yell and scream if something goes wrong with my travel plans.

__ **Yes** __ **No** __ **Sometimes**

6. People think you are powerful if you are not afraid to show how angry you are with the service that you receive.

__ **Yes** __ **No** __ **Sometimes**

7. Watch out when I'm behind the wheel. I am a determined driver.

__ **Yes** __ **No** __ **Sometimes**

8. When I'm driving is one of the few times that I really feel IN CONTROL!

__ **Yes** __ **No** __ **Sometimes**

9. Speed limits get in my way.

__ Yes __ No __ Sometimes

Strategies for Dealing
with Vampire Behavior

Discounting Manners

1. Analyze how you feel about your meal times.

2. Could a more tranquil meal time bring a more relaxed dimension to you life?

3. Review the ten top dining mistakes to make certain that you are not guilty of using any of them when you dine.

4. Are you aware of which utensils to use when you are dining? Is this information of importance to you?

5. How do you treat your family, friends and co-workers, particularly when you are having a rough day?

6. Do you enjoy travel, or do you often find the experience frustrating? Plan specific ways to relieve your stress such as having a book to read, allowing extra time, having small bills and change for tips and necessities.

7. Remember that you are often observed in stressful situations. An unpleasant encounter may influence how others perceive you. (An important speaker was not asked to speak again due to the manner in which he treated the check-in staff at the hotel.)

8. Curb "road rage." If you are guilty of using this behavior, find out why, and take steps to correct your road warrior habits.

9. Allow plenty of time for your commute. Structure your commute to avoid rush hour traffic whenever it is possible to do so.

10. Avoid closely scheduled back-to-back meetings when time in traffic is required. Allow a cushion of time in order to keep calm if something happens to the time frame, or if a change in the time frame is desired.

Vampire Quotient Quiz

If You've Been Bitten By a Vampire

Discounting Manners

Answer YES, NO, or SOMETIMES to any of the following questions. Use the quiz to evaluate whether you have been "bitten" by a vampire. You have it within your power to make changes in your behavior in order to avoid these "bites."

1. I feel uncomfortable when someone pushes their plate aside at the table.

   __ Yes __ No __ Sometimes

2. I cannot enjoy my meal when someone I am eating with is using poor manners.

   __ Yes __ No __ Sometimes

3. I distance myself from individuals in a group who make smacking noises when eating.

   __ Yes __ No __ Sometimes

4. I question the education level of people with poor table manners.

   __ **Yes** __ **No** __ **Sometimes**

5. I feel intimidated when I don't know which eating utensils to use when dining with others.

   __ **Yes** __ **No** __ **Sometimes**

6. My family, friends and co-workers don't give me enough respect.

   __ **Yes** __ **No** __ **Sometimes**

7. People tend to talk to me when I want to sleep on the airplane.

   __ **Yes** __ **No** __ **Sometimes**

8. People in other cars on the road often cut in front of me when I am driving.

   __ **Yes** __ **No** __ **Sometimes**

Strategies for Avoiding

Vampire Bites

Discounting Manners

1. Assume that other people's actions are not always directed at you.

2. Avoid eating with people who have table manners that you find offensive. If these people are family members share your concerns about their behavior.

3. Set the stage by creating esthetic eating experiences for your family in your meal preparation and dining.

4. Be a terrific example by using correct table manners if proper eating etiquette is of prime importance to you.

5. Treat your family, friends and co-workers in the same way that you would like to be treated.

6. Speak up if someone is invading your personal space by talking to you or annoying you during travel.

7. Avoid high traffic times when you are traveling by automobile if at all possible.

8. Make certain that you are using your car signals correctly when you are driving.

Chapter Ten: Vampire Attitude

Sharpen Your Fangs– Avoid High-Tech Faux Pas

Everything is going faster these days. We can get an instant replay of the war. We can receive breaking news information immediately. We can use a computer to learn about a variety of topics very quickly. We can send notification of an event rapidly over the Internet.

It used to take several office workers and an executive to issue a report along with an extra day to prepare it. These days everything goes a lot faster and fewer people are needed for the effort. High speed everything is in demand and people want even faster sources of information. There is a "Star Wars" bombardment of information as well as the need on the part of the public to receive instant answers and further information that they request. Even the current speeds of information aren't fast enough for some and new technologies offer even faster transfer.

All of these new high-tech trends have caused some of the population to become frantic as they try to keep up with the changes. Vampires are having an opportunity for attacks in the free wheeling open range of high technology.

Computers, E-mail and Fax Machines

Turn on your computer and go. Computers are here to stay and are totally marvelous. When you know the whistles and bells to make them operate effectively you can work miracles. When you have a computer "blow up" or "crash" you may definitely think that vampires are at work in your computer.

There are highway bandit vampires that come across your computer screen in the form of uninvited viruses. Junk mail is also one of the vampire computer hazards that invades your screen. Your e-mail address may be a blessing or a scourge in keeping you at your screen answering, reading and clearing e-mails. E-mail etiquette is a topic in these times. Many people who send you an e-mail have a definite expectation of receiving an answer or an acknowledgement that the e-mail was received. They expect this acknowledgement in a 24 hour turn around. Many people think that sending an e-mail insures that the person to whom it was sent receives it. This is not always the case. It is proper to request an acknowledgement that the e-mail was received.

Some people use the channel of e-mail in order to request information. They should include their address, telephone number, fax number and any other information that would be pertinent to a reply or response.

A response is not always required to e-mail, particularly unsolicited junk e-mail or advertising e-mail that is not requested by the owner of the computer. Do respond to people that you know or to those that you have personally solicited for some particular reason.

Be cautious of forwarding the messages of others. Do not share the e-mail addresses of others when forwarding messages.

Fax machines offer another option for the transfer of information. When you are sending a fax, be certain to include a cover sheet with the proper information.

Don't assume that a fax has been received just because you sent it. Request a message telling you that the fax was received.

Respect areas of privacy when sending fax messages. In some corporations, a fax will come into the office in a general area. Others will have the opportunity to read the fax should they choose to do so.

Professional Voice Mail

Some of the voice mail messages that are received by callers to professionals could make a vampire shudder. "I am away from my desk, or with a client," was one of the first messages that was often used when voice mail came into existence. Obviously, when a caller receives your voice mail you are not available. The caller doesn't really care where you are, but they do care to know when they might hear from you. Messages like, "Today is January 21st. I will be in and out of the office and do check my voice mail each hour or daily. I will return your call promptly." Give the caller hope that they will hear from you in a timely fashion. They also know that you are operating in the present since you have given them the day or the week's review.

Leaving a voice mail also requires responsibility. Speak slowly and leave your name. Tell why you are calling and request a return call at a time that may be convenient for you. If your call needs a response by a particular time, indicate this information without being abrasive. Always repeat your name and telephone number twice so that the caller will be sure to receive your message without noise interference.

The turn-around time on returning telephone calls is 24 hours. The return of telephone calls in a prompt fashion is appreciated by callers who are trying to reach you.

> "The more customized **your approach** is to your audience, **the better** you'll do."
>
> Bill Brooks, *Niche Selling*

Cell Phones

They are everywhere. Few places are sacred from the cell phone. It will be interesting to see if cell phones become banned in particular areas. This trend already has occurred on airplanes. People are told to turn off cell phones in concerts and special performances. Some states talk about banning cell phone conversation in automobiles. Common sense should be used when talking on cell phones. There are times that others may be disturbed by being forced to listen to your conversation.

Phone Conversations

Phone conversations are times when we are directly connected to others. If you have "vampire tendencies" on the telephone and your caller feels "bitten," that person may not choose to speak with you again. Phone solicitors are having real difficulty in many instances because of their lack of etiquette. Various types of phone blocking techniques are being invented because people do not want to be interrupted during meal times or during other times when they are busy with their families. Be aware of proper phone manners when you are making and receiving calls.

It is important to note that people are making calls to friends, family and associates all over the world. Learn what the time zones are for the people that you are calling, and respect the appropriate business hours for talking on the telephone.

Vampire Quotient Quiz

for Vampire Tendencies

Sharpen Your Fangs–
Avoid High-Tech Faux Pas

Answer YES, NO, or SOMETIMES to any of the following questions. If the majority of your answers are YES, you may have vampire tendencies. If you feel that you do have vampire tendencies, take steps to see what you can do to improve your behavior.

1. I forward an e-mail without thinking if the sender wanted it repeated.

   __ Yes __ No __ Sometimes

2. I always assume that sent e-mails and faxes reach their intended destinations.

   __ Yes __ No __ Sometimes

3. I send inappropriate messages on e-mail.

   __ Yes __ No __ Sometimes

4. I may be eating when I am talking to others on the phone.

   __ Yes __ No __ Sometimes

5. I put callers on hold when I am alerted by my call waiting signal.

__ Yes __ No __ Sometimes

6. I read the e-mails and faxes of other people whenever I have a chance to do so.

__ Yes __ No __ Sometimes

7. I don't go to much effort to take phone messages for others. My interest is not there if the phone message is not for me.

__ Yes __ No __ Sometimes

8. I talk on my cell phone when I feel like doing so. I don't want to miss any important calls.

__ Yes __ No __ Sometimes

Strategies for Dealing
with Vampire Behavior

Sharpen Your Fangs– Avoid High-Tech Faux Pas

1. Learn as much as you can about using your computer to your advantage.
2. Use correct grammar, punctuation, greetings and closings when you are communicating by e-mail.
3. Understand how to protect your computer from uninvited viruses.
4. Do not open attachments from people that you do not know, or in e-mails where there is no greeting or when the greeting is a generic one.
5. Do not forward the e-mail address books of e-mails that you receive from other people.
6. Avoid sending offensive remarks about others in your e-mail communications.
7. Check to see that e-mails and faxes reach their intended destinations.
8. Avoid eating, chewing, or other interruptions that may occur when you are speaking on the phone to others.

9. Take messages for others as you would hope that others would take them for you.

10. Respect the privacy of others when using your cell phone.

11. Avoid yelling to a person in your home when you are talking on the telephone. Let the people in your home know that you will be talking on the phone so that they will not summon you by yelling.

12. It is never appropriate to take a phone call when you are with a client. Your attention should be directed to the person who is with you.

Vampire Quotient Quiz

If You've Been Bitten By a Vampire

Sharpen Your Fangs–
Avoid High-Tech Faux Pas

Answer YES, NO, or SOMETIMES to any of the following questions. If you answer YES to most of these questions, you may have been "bitten" by a vampire. Figure out how to avoid "vampire bites" or how to educate those who are the offenders.

1. Callers do not leave their name when leaving a message.

   __ Yes   __ No   __ Sometimes

2. I do not receive replies to some of the e-mails I send.

   __ Yes   __ No   __ Sometimes

3. I hear the children of people that I am speaking to yelling in the background.

   __ Yes   __ No   __ Sometimes

4. People put me “on hold” when they receive another call.

__ **Yes** __ **No** __ **Sometimes**

5. My associates use their cell phones when we are having a conversation.

__ **Yes** __ **No** __ **Sometimes**

6. I don’t know how to avoid callers who talk “on and on.”

__ **Yes** __ **No** __ **Sometimes**

7. I find it difficult to set boundaries for myself when talking about the problems of others.

__ **Yes** __ **No** __ **Sometimes**

8. I become overwhelmed in trying to handle the e-mail requests of others.

__ **Yes** __ **No** __ **Sometimes**

9. I become frozen in clearing my e-mails.

__ **Yes** __ **No** __ **Sometimes**

10. I become angry when someone dials my cell phone in error and I let them know it.

__ **Yes** __ **No** __ **Sometimes**

Strategies for Avoiding
Vampire Bites

Sharpen Your Fangs– Avoid High-Tech Faux Pas

1. It is always polite to return phone calls. If you are lacking information (such as name or reason for calling) clarify it when you return the call.

2. Keep requesting information regarding the delivery of your e-mail messages. Remember that the "squeaky" wheel gets the oil.

3. When you are on the phone with children screaming in the background, request a possible time that would be appropriate for your conversation.

4. If someone suggests that they need to pick up a call when you are the one that was there first, request that they call back when they have completed their call. Do not consent to remain on hold.

5. Let your associates know that you would appreciate their not talking on their cell phones when you are in their company.

6. When you receive a call from someone who has no sense of time, qualify the time that you have to spend on the call at the beginning of the conversation.

7. Have a timer by your phone. Allow a five or ten minute time window to hear about your friend's problems.

8. Don't become a victim of "e-mail control." Read e-mails when you have time to do so. Answer them one by one. You do not have to be superman or superwoman.

9. Do not keep someone on hold for longer than 30 seconds. If you must take a call, ask if you can call them back at a time convenient for them.

10. E-mail communication can come across in a negative, impersonal manner. Imagine how you would view your message if you were the reader.

Afterword

We hope you have discovered whether you have "vampire tendencies" or whether you have been bitten by "vampire people." The tests in the book were informal guidelines to help you decide what is happening in your life, how you communicate to others, and if you need assistance with your own communication.

If you have discovered that you are too much of a vampire person, you may wish to curb your vampire-like tendencies. Only you can make the decision to change your behavior. When you make an effort to treat other people better, you will be quite surprised how much better they will treat you.

If you are one who is often "bitten" by a vampire, you may want to review why these bites happen. Do you allow the pain to continue by refusing to take the necessary actions to change your behavior? Do you continually find too many "vampire people" in your life? You may wish to discover new friends and associates who value you as a person.

"Kindness is more than deeds. It is an attitude, an expression, a look, a touch. It is anything that lifts another person."

C. Neil Strait

The major focus of the book is about respecting other people. Sometimes we become "too full of ourselves" and focus entirely on who we are, how we feel, and what we want. The following poems are worth sharing, to help all of us keep a better perspective and image of ourselves.

PROPER PERSPECTIVE

Sometime, when you're feeling important!
Sometime, when your ego's in bloom;
Sometime, when you take for granted
You're the most qualified in the room;

Sometime, when you feel your going
Would leave an unfilled hole,
Just follow these simple instructions,
And see how it humbles your soul.

Take a bucket and fill it with water;
Put your hand in it right to the wrist;
Pull it out and the hole that's remaining
Is a measure of how you'll be missed.

You may splash all you please when you enter,
You can stir up the water galore.
But, stop and you'll find in a minute
That it looks quite the same as before.

The moral in this quaint example,
Is do just the best that you can,
Be proud of yourself, but remember,
There's no indispensable man.

Anonymous

A Little Walk Around Yourself

When you're criticizing others and are
finding here and there
A fault or two to speak of, or a weakness
you can tear;
When you're blaming someone's meanness
and accusing one of pelf–
It's time that you went out and take a walk
around yourself.

There's lots of human failures in the
average of us all,
And lots of grave shortcomings in the
short ones and the tall;
But, when we think of evils men should
lay upon the shelves,
It's time we all went out and take a walk
around ourselves.

We need so often in this life
this balancing of scales.
This seeing how much in us wins and
how much in us fails;
Before you judge another– just to lay
him on a shelf–
It would be a splendid plan to take a
walk around yourself.

Helen Welshimer

Do all the good you can
By all the means you can
In all the ways you can
In all the places you can
At all the times you can
To all the people you can
As long as ever you can!

John Wesley

About the Authors

Debra Lindquist, MA, CIP, has been in the image consulting industry since 1970. She is the owner of the premier color design system, Color Profiles, Ltd. which was created in 1974. Debra is the author of *The Color Consultant's Handbook* and has written a number of articles for various image publications. She chose wardrobes and makeup for over forty make-over articles in *The Rocky Mountain News.* She was a stylist for a segment of the national television program, 20/20 called "Creating Your Best First Impression." Debra has been a member of National Speakers Association. She is a speaker and a trainer.

Joyce M. Knudsen, Ph.D., CIM, is internationally known for her Home Study Certification Mentoring Program, which offers International Image Certification, with clients in the U.S., Asia, Europe, and South America. Joyce "listens" to client needs and helps them to "design their own program." She is Founder and President of The ImageMaker, Inc. (www.imagemaker1.com) and is a recipient of Certified Image Master (CIM) from The Association of Image Consultants International. Joyce is also the IMMIE Award Winner of the Image Makers Merit of Industry Excellence.

To contact Debra Lindquist or Joyce Knudsen,
please call:

1-888-845-5600
or e-mail:
Debra Lindquist – llindquist@prodigy.net
Joyce Knudsen – optimist44@aol.com